BEAUTY IN THE BATTLE

Stormproof

Stories Compiled by

NICOLE JONES

Copyright 2021 Nicole Jones

All rights reserved. In accordance with U.S. Copyright Act of 1976, the scanning, uploading, and electronic sharing of any part of this book without permission of the author is unlawful piracy and theft of the author's intellectual property.

Contents

Introduction 1

1. Gracefully Broken 3
2. The Only Voice That Matters.. 9
3. When God Says Something Different for Your life 15
4. Who Told You That?.. 21
5. David, Take the Call!... 27
6. (Un)forgiven 33
7. The Pieces of My Heart 39
8. Real Love (Unconditionally) 45
9. Overcoming a Loyalty of Lies... 51
10. It's Time… 57
11. Embracing My Ausome World 63
12. Looking Ahead.. 69
13. Will You Abort, Miscarry, or Birth 77
14. Who Cares for the Caregiver?... 83
15. From Check Him to Check Me 89
16. I Am Okay with Me.. 95

17. Secure Your Own Mask Before Helping Others 101

18. Around this Mountain 107

19. The Secret Key: How it Unlocked My New Life 113

20. Finding Me…One Unexpected Adventure after Another. 121

Introduction

There are times in life when it seems like all hell literally breaks loose against you and you begin to ponder your destiny. Out of nowhere, winds of circumstances start blowing you back as you try to take a step forward. Cold and heavy rains of defeat start pouring and pounding down on you so much that you can't even think. The ground starts to crumble beneath you, pulling you deeper and deeper into a pit of depression.

No matter what, life doesn't let up. You are in a storm—a storm for your life. A storm rises against you and is trying with everything in its power to destroy you. And it doesn't matter if the storm is physical, medical, financial, or professional. But despite all of that, you can still reach within yourself and find something that keeps you going, which gives you the strength to face life.

This book is a collection of true, raw, real-life stories of situations and storms. The women in this book endured the waves of disappointment, shame, guilt, and fear of getting to their shores of truth and freedom. Here you will read about how they all had to put on their "life preservers" of hope and faith; and ride the waves of the storms in their lives.

Storms occur to everyone and in every season of life. When you are determined that NOTHING can stop you, you find a way to push ahead and fight through! You could literally walk through a tornado and come out on the other side unharmed and unscathed with grace. You become like the authors of this book, ***Stormproof.***

• CHAPTER 1 •

Gracefully Broken

What does it really mean to be "gracefully broken?" When I think of being gracefully broken, I think about going through something that hurts you to your core, something that makes you feel you will never get over or get through, BUT you do, and you do so through unwavering faith. It's going through a process that only God can get you through, and you have to trust Him completely, not knowing what the outcome will be. This process breaks you in every way, but at the same time, you come out stronger, better, and as pure gold.

Allowing God to break you is not an easy thing to go through. Right before my breaking process, I remember saying to God, "God let Your will be done in my life, nothing more, nothing less, nothing else. It is well with my soul." At that point, I was in an abusive marriage. My now ex-husband was verbally, mentally, emotionally, and financially abusive. He was a manipulator and a liar. We had two young kids together, and I had to decide to stay in a marriage where my husband was abusive and cheating or to pack up and leave with my two boys. I chose the latter.

I wanted a healthier life for my boys and me. I didn't want them growing up thinking it was okay to treat people that way. When I left, I had nothing. A friend gave me a gas card and money to get my boys food for the road. My family lived in another state. I had no job because I was a stay-at-home mom, but I knew I had to go. I moved my two boys in with my mom, and I started over. It was hard moving back home with my mom. I felt I should have been in a different place in my life and let so many people down by being in that situation. But oh, did I grow in that place.

I went on to go through a slanderous divorce. My ex-husband lied to so many people, including the judge, but I didn't care. I wanted out of that marriage and what was fair for my boys. God was with me every step of the way, and He came through for me every time. I remember the first day of court God gave me the scripture Exodus 14:14 (The Lord will fight for you; you need only be still) and the very last day when we signed our divorce papers; God reminded me by that being my verse of the day in my Bible app.

One thing we have to know and understand, it's okay to be broken. Admitting your brokenness allows God to come in and do His work in you. When you are in a broken state, God can come in, heal and remove all the things that hold you bamck from where He needs to take you. In my broken state, I went to a counselor to talk through my pain. (I highly recommend getting counseling or coaching when going through any trial.) The healing process God took me through was one I never knew I needed. I confronted my pain right in the face and let it know that it wasn't going to control my life. I made a DECISION to be healed for myself and my boys.

Once I confronted my pain, I decided to let it go, and I forgave my ex-husband for all the hurt, lies, manipulation, and everything else that caused me pain. I also forgave myself for allowing the pain for so long and not thinking I deserved better. I didn't realize the weight and burdens I was carrying until the day I laid them all down. I gave them back to Jesus, and I was able to breathe. I remember exhaling like never before. Once I got to a place where I forgave my ex-husband and myself, I dropped that heavy load, and I was able to bless him. Yep, you read that right. I began to pray for my ex-husband and asked God to bless him. He no longer controlled me. I was no longer affected by his lies, and the pain melted away. I was moving in a new direction towards my purpose.

I am a believer that you can turn your pain into your purpose. While going through my divorce, I decided to get my certification to become a Life Coach. I began helping others while I was still going through my pain. It helped me to continue my personal journey towards healing and growth. When you allow God to use your pain to help others, you grow and continue to heal. I am not only a certified Life Coach, but I am a speaker, author, and teacher. I offer courses that help people in their relationships, divorce, healing, or just finding their purpose.

God can heal every broken piece in your life and turn it into something beautiful. He said He would give us beauty for ashes, and He's doing just that in my life. And guess what? He's not done yet, and I am here for this journey.

RaChell Crowe is the founder of *Marriage Unstoppable and Life Unstoppable Coaching LLC.* She is a Life Coach, author, speaker, and most importantly, a mom to two wonderful boys. God gave RaChell the marriage ministry during a time when she faced trials in her marriage.

She developed a passion to see marriages live and thrive despite her own marriage coming to a tragic end. RaChell has turned her pain into her passion by helping others heal and have thriving relationships.

• CHAPTER 2 •

The Only Voice That Matters

"There's nothing wrong with that boy; he just needs a whooping…"
"Leave him with me; I'll teach him how to act."
"He doesn't look autistic."
"They didn't call it autism when I was coming up…"
"He only acts like that when he's with you…"
"If the teacher is so busy dealing with him, what about the other kids…"

The problem was that as harsh as they sounded, I believed all those remarks said to me in the early years of parenting my son to be true. I was not consistent with my discipline and not good at setting boundaries. My son did act differently around other authority figures than he did around me. If autism has a look, it means when looking at my son, you could not tell that he was any different from any other typical boy.

My son's behaviors did keep his teacher from focusing on the other kids in the classroom, and he was a big distraction to their learning. He hit and threw things at kids, and he may have even bit one; all of this was true. From the outside looking in, it was easy to assume that I was a lazy or overwhelmed mother in dire need of their advice and good counsel, and if I would just listen to all of them, then everything would be alright. However, I decided to be open about what I was experiencing and feeling as a parent and sought outside help.

When the diagnosis came, the psychiatrist was not nice about it. He scared me, not just me, but all the parents in the room that evening when we were told what life would be like parenting a child on the autism spectrum. He said they would lack eye-contact and value for social connections and that they would be under our care for life, not to expect grandchildren or for them ever to get married. We should discourage relationships with the opposite sex altogether because they will not know how to handle the emotions that follow. He also told us not to expect them to graduate from high school with a real diploma or to be able to hold a regular job - just menial tasks with minimal interaction with people.

Say whatever you want about this doctor's methods, but one thing was for certain. Whatever he wrote in his report giving Todd's complete diagnosis ensured that my son would have the best services, with no interruption, and no one ever questioning or changing them, no matter where we moved in the country. Through all of this, how was I doing? My professional goals were put on hold because I was in fear of having a job that would require more of what I could give. My parenting life suffered as my daughter was very active in everything from softball to Girl Scouts, so I ran myself ragged, trying to make sure she did not lose out on having a fulfilling childhood. My spiritual life suffered since the church we attended was not equipped to handle a child with special needs, and special needs ministries were just not a thing then. My social life suffered, as I did not have a lot of free time to cultivate my friendships, and whenever we were invited as a family to events, that time was interrupted because of Todd's social limitations. My mental health was suffering because little did I know, I was sinking into a depression.

What have I learned? Although it was difficult, I gained many skills: developing structure and schedules, successful co-parenting, cherishing my "me-time" and developing an identity outside of motherhood, how to be a parent advocate, and that people, sometimes the closest people to you, will have you doubting yourself and God's purpose for your life. Most importantly, I learned Todd's language and started listening to his voice. His voice became the only one that mattered to me. My turning point came when I realized how comfortable Todd was in his skin. Of course, like most parents with kids on the autism spectrum, I spent the first few years of his diagnosis trying to find a cure. One day, Todd said to me in his way, "I like me; I don't want to change." I knew then that my focus and my strategy had to change. I changed what I was reading, to whom I was listening, and I started to place similar expectations on him that I gave his older sister. My language also had to change. My voice inflection changed when I talked to him. How I used to describe him changed, he wasn't autistic; he was a child with autism. I learned how to dream and how to let Todd have dreams too; dreams that have no limits. Todd has given himself his own set of dreams and goals, and even though some seem big to me, he has become the picture for me that nothing is too big for God. I knew that God made me his mother for a reason, and it was not to bring him harm, but to be his most prominent voice and advocate.

I shiver at what Todd's life would look like had I believed those powerful, influential voices in every other area in my life. If I would have let those voices put me down and hold me completely responsible for my son's diagnosis, I am doubtful that I would have the self-assured, confident, independent young man I have today. He has much life left and is slowly checking off on the list of things he will never do that Dr. L. gave him so many years before. Right before we moved out of state, almost seven years after his diagnosis, Todd and I visited Dr. L. He looked him straight in the eyes, shook his hand, and said, "Hello, Doctor. My name is Todd."

Besides being a wife and mother, Lena Marie Irish is a non-profit professional, child and special needs advocate, and community volunteer. She recently went back to school and completed her MBA with the hopes of creating meaningful career opportunities within Corporate America for people with developmental disabilities.

Also, she is extremely passionate about helping anyone who does not feel like they are not being heard, to be heard. Lena moved from the San Francisco Bay Area to the metro Atlanta area in 2007 with her two children, Nia and Todd. She met and later married Edgar, and they now have a blended family of five kids and Cocoa, the chocolate lab. She gets her inspiration from Christ and seeks to follow where He leads her in life.

• CHAPTER 3 •

When God Says Something Different for Your Life

The storms that tried to blow me away actually made me stronger than most. Like many people who have faced storms in their lives, the first question that comes to mind is, "Why me, Lord?" Well, I can remember asking that question so many times in my life until He was like, "Because I knew that only you would be able to help people when I sent them to you. It would be your words and your testimony that would encourage them to know that if I did it for you, I would do it for them as well." However, it was not until I became an adult with children that I started to see that everything I faced, was to make me more compassionate for people who had also been hurt. It seems as if God made me a magnet for people that need someone to speak life into their situation. Someone who would listen to the hurt they have faced when others would have told them to get over it.

The storms I have faced molded me into who I am today. I've faced several storms such as childhood abandonment from my parents to child molestation and emotional abuse. Most people who have dealt with these types of storms have demons that follow them when they become adults, to the point that they just let them take over their lives. I am grateful that this was not my story. I was able to rebuke the demons that lived in my head in the name of Jesus. When I thought of killing myself and throwing in the towel, God spoke to me and said He was not done with my story. The emotional demon is the worst of them all, because it controls your thoughts. This one made me feel like I was less of a person. It was the voice of a family member, which I overheard in a conversation with another family member. The conversation went a little like this; "I do not want her here." They also said things like, I would grow up to be nothing if I left, or that I would get pregnant and drop out of high school.

I think that out of all the things that people told me while growing up, like I was ugly, stupid, and everything in between, that was the one phrase that made me fight to prove that person wrong. I know it is easier to say, "Why care what people say, just live your life." It hurts because I was their child before certain life-changing events happened in their lives. I felt safe, and I felt loved most of all. However, after the events took place, I felt the same way the little girl did when her mother and father left her, abandoned and unloved. I do not think people ever truly understand the effects that their words have.

As a child, we would always say, "Sticks and stones may break my bones, but words will never hurt me." I think what we meant was, you might see the bruises from sticks and stones, but you may not see the underlying damage words cause. In other words, words hurt worse than bruises because at least bruises do heal with time. Although these hurtful words stayed with me in my mind growing up, I had to learn to use them for good and not for bad. I had to reprogram my brain. I thought the key to reprogramming was doing the opposite of what others had to say. I had to find God. I prayed like no one else, and I asked Him to use me.

Well, they say be careful what you pray for, and that's exactly what I learned. The first prayer was for God to make me whole, loving, and understanding. He did just that! I left everything that I was used to and started a new journey in a big city. I looked at this as an opportunity to reinvent myself and to become the best person that I could be. I wanted to find my true purpose in life. I started a new school where I wouldn't be judged because of my physical appearance, or my family tree. For the first time, I was able to breathe. I graduated with a 3.2 GPA, so that part of the demon was dead. However, I did get pregnant during my freshman year of college, and that's when the devil tried me extra hard. I started thinking all kinds of thoughts like "what will people say?" or "what will my family say?" and "how am I going to make this work?" I remember talking to God at that moment and saying to Him, "I can barely take care of myself, and now I am having a baby to take care of too!" "And in this crazy world!" I was terrified. It was so bad that my grades that semester were worse than I could have imagined. I remember saying to myself; maybe they were right… I won't become anything in life, and I should just quit. But when I gave birth to my son, the tune of shame in my head was over. I looked into his eyes and said, "You will never feel the pain that I felt."

God changed me at that moment for good. He had given me a chance to give the love that I wanted, to someone else—a chance to erase all the curses that had been placed in my life. The struggles I had before I had my son disappeared, and life became easier. He placed people in my life that spoke words of encouragement to me, and I will never forget all He has and will continue to do for me.

Shonta Holt Mitchell was born in the city; however, she grew up in a small rural town. She received her education in the public school system. After graduating from high school, she received her bachelor's degree in business administration and her master's in accounting.

She has vast experience in the work environment, from customer service to finance. She enjoys spending quality time with her family, friends, and sharing positive thoughts to help make life easier for others. She is a firm believer that there's some good in everything that seems to be bad. Her future goal is to establish a foundation that will help young mothers and children flee from abuse.

• CHAPTER 4 •

Who Told You That?

Who told you that you would never be able to do it? Who told you that you were not capable of achieving everything you put your mind to? Who told you what being successful was? Who told you to choose money over peace? What is your first memory of these thoughts? Whenever you first heard any of this, it began to mold and shape your life. It was like indelible ink into your soul, shaping who you would ultimately become. As a young girl, I was groomed for success. I recall my parents making sure I was well-spoken, well educated, knew how to care for the home, was business savvy, and I would always have a *good job*.

I did not take the route that my parents, family, or friends considered conventional. I went to college and majored in Agribusiness. Agribusiness? Yes, Agribusiness! I did not know what it was when presented to me either, but I had to go to college and get a degree, and this major offered a scholarship. I received my degree and immediately began working. My first job would be in management for a major retail company. Although I hated it, I finished their training program in nine months instead of the twelve they projected. Don't forget that I was trained to exceed standards.

Once I finished the program, I quit and moved to another state without a job. Oh my, how could I do that? No one would understand, but I still moved. I was in the new city for only two weeks before I landed a banking job. I worked in banking, customer service for an alarm company, benefits for a few major companies, with some temporary assignments and part-time gigs in between. Over the years, I have always managed to have employment to sustain my lifestyle. I have had some high-paying salaries, as well as some almost minimum wage-paying jobs. Some much better than others, but I was employed. I endured some extremely stressful situations and some incompetent managers who made my life a living HELL. But I was taught that you could not quit a job without another job, no matter how bad the job was. There was no consideration of mental health. That irritated my entire soul.

In September 2019, I quit the job I had been in for two years. I took the job after getting another degree because I thought it was the next step in the trajectory of my career. Boy, was I wrong! Sixty days in, and I knew I had made the biggest mistake; but I could not quit. I made a decent salary and had a senior-level title, but I was **MISERABLE**! I dealt with racism, classism, and colorism. I was micromanaged because of the insecurities of the manager who had never managed before. The environment became so unbearable. I had anxiety, depression, and became physically ill. The day I left, I clearly heard God say, ***"Leave and live, or stay and die."*** I finished the day and left them in a good place. I took my things to my car (I had been taking stuff all along because it just didn't feel right), turned in my badge, gave the resignation letter to HR, and left.

I went home to an apartment that I had been in for only a little while. I had enough money saved to last a few months. Then the bottom fell out. I was broke, unemployed, on food stamps, and had to move in with my mother. I slept on my mother's couch for almost a year. I was embarrassed and went through a myriad of emotions. Then I decided that I would not let the fact that I chose MY LIFE over a job killing me, keep me down. I applied for more jobs than I could keep track of. I was turned down for several jobs that I know I was highly qualified for. It was God's protection, because COVID happened. Many of the jobs were connected to hospitality and folded.

There was one job that I applied for, but due to COVID, I was notified that it was placed on hold. A few months later, I received an email inviting me to interview for the job. I accepted the interview and knew it was the one. I had a few more interviews, but no response. One Friday, I was having a breakdown and telling God how unfair it all was. I was ready to give up. Little did I know, I was already offered the job. The email never showed up in my inbox.

The following Monday, I received an email stating I had until the next day to accept the offer. I contacted the company and was sent another letter. I accepted, and I do not regret it. It was not the money that I expected, but peace of mind does not have a price. Lest I forget, during the time of unemployment and even with a lower salary, I paid off a student loan, two credit cards, and moved into my own place. Proverbs 29:25 in The Message Bible says, "The fear of human opinion disables; trusting in God protects you from that." Simply stated, don't worry about the opinions of people when you know your actions are God-ordained.

People will have you believe that you will fail every time, but you can do ALL things with God! God made you perfectly, in His image. There is no need to feel inadequate about any circumstance or situation this life of smoke, mirrors, and lies may throw your way. You have not missed out. It's not too late; everything is in God's timing. But remember, He's INFINITE. We're the ones operating on a schedule. Be encouraged and know that YOU ARE ENOUGH.

Sherrie L. Charles is the CEO and owner of *TVIC Enterprises, LLC.* Professionally, she is an educator and adult learning facilitator. By purpose, she is a minister and certified professional Life Coach who has walked through her journey. The gems Sherrie has acquired along the way are a part of her ministry and coaching strategy. She utilizes her testimony to impact the lives of others.

• CHAPTER 5 •

David, Take the Call!

What happens when you create your own storm? Often in life, we're faced with countless decisions and spend time agonizing over the right thing to do. No one wants the weight of making the wrong decision on their shoulders, so we struggle with second-guessing and overthinking so much to the point that we cause our own storms. Hearing from God is one thing but moving on what you heard can be challenging at times. Particularly, when what God says makes no sense!

In June 2020, during the pandemic, I sensed God telling me to quit my job. His exact words were "Turn in a two-week notice." It was odd because I knew this job would be stable in the pandemic as we were constantly hiring. I was a Regional Recruiter over two regions and a few startups. Even though that level of stability was there, the company had reduced our pay by 20% as a cost-saving measure. I heard it again and even told a dear friend what I'd heard. Yet, I didn't move. I found myself trying to negotiate and bargain with God. I would say things like, "God, let me finish this project and I'll give my notice." I had just been put on this startup project in Chicago, which was demanding, and the deadline was close to impossible. I wanted to launch the Chicago project, and then I'd give notice. Reasonable, right? Now, if you know anything about God, you know that He means what He says, even though He's loving and compassionate towards us.

We all know the story of Jonah when God told him to go to Nineveh. Jonah didn't, he chose to go to Tarshish instead, got swallowed up by a whale, lived to tell about it, and ended up going to Nineveh anyway. Just like God had initially told him. When we read this story, our first thought is always, "Why didn't Jonah just do what God told him to do the first time?" Jonah would not have been in the boat on the way to Tarshish, which got caught in a storm, which led to him being kicked off the boat by the other passengers had he just done what God told him to do! Just as Jonah's storm resulted from him not obeying God's instruction, many of our storms result from the same thing.

The Chicago project was my Tarshish; and when God told me to turn in a two-week notice in June, I should have just trusted His instruction. The company prematurely spent $80 million on new equipment before being awarded the Chicago contract to solidify them as the bid's best provider. In other words, they wanted to show they had the equipment needed to win the project. This would have proven to be a smart move and quite beneficial, but 2020 was the pandemic height. Spending that type of money when customer usage and revenue were down was risky. From the first project meeting, I knew it wouldn't succeed. I can be extremely optimistic at times, but I am a realist every time. We were given a September deadline to hire one hundred fifty people. One hundred and fifty people, in the middle of the pandemic, with no guarantee that they would start work in September. Although I voiced my concern as the lead on the project, I forged ahead and tried to keep my team motivated as much as possible.

I continued to hear, "Turn in a two-week notice." I planned to resign right after the project; however, God had different plans. He'd given me a Nineveh assignment. Weeks passed, and our numbers were falling more and more behind as the September 9th deadline approached. Leadership was more demanding of my team and insisted that I micromanage the process. I couldn't lead my team to believe in something I didn't believe in myself. Being on countless conference calls about something that would never materialize was torture. I asked God for relief, and the relief came one Friday morning when my VP, whom I never had a problem with, started taking his frustration out on me. At that moment, with about twenty-five other people on a TEAMS call, I knew what was happening. This was my "belly of the whale" moment.

As he was yelling, I spoke these words to my immediate boss, David, who was also on the call. "David, take the call!" I had to speak up because the VP kept overtalking. Again, I said, "David, take the call!" I was very calm but clear. I hung up the call and typed an immediate letter of resignation. I'd never done anything so badass in my life! I quit! Over the remainder of the day, I kept hearing God say, "I'm so proud of you." That was on a Friday. The following Monday, three days later, I was offered a new and higher position, and my salary was restored. My salary was almost doubled! God needed my skillset on this new venture. He set this whole thing up to put a spirit in my VP that forced me to move! Three days later, He placed me right where I needed to be. God knew all along what His intent was, and the tumultuous summer I had was the result of me not following His original instruction.

It's true, storms rise to make us stronger, but we create many storms through our disobedience. Like Jonah, I created my belly of the whale experience. "David, take the call" was one of the most courageous things I'd done. It renewed my faith in God and renewed trust in Him even when the thing He asks you to do makes no sense. Know this, God always has a plan. And His plan and "Nineveh" for your life will always be much better than anything you can imagine.

Nicole Jones is a creative and Kingdom-centered Influencer who embodies crazy, supernatural faith in every aspect of her life. Nicole's down-to-earth yet practical and direct delivery reaches people at their core, yielding transformation and healing in everyone she encounters.

Nicole understands what it is to be stuck, frustrated, and disappointed. She inspires and empowers others to do the same leveraging spirit and truth to bring transformative healing into the world! In her heart is a desire for everyone to win fueled by love and compassion.

Nicole uses her truth, spiritual growth, and self-awareness to empower others to evolve and become the most-highest form of themselves so they too can impact the world. She is a VP of Human Resources in her professional life and a mom of three grown children.

• CHAPTER 6 •

(Un)forgiven

Well, you have finally made it to my chapter! This story is not one I share often. It is so painfully personal that I did not want to tell it to myself. However, pieces of the past would resurface and disrupt my present by reopening old wounds that I had pretended to be healed from. Ultimately, instead of running from my truth, I need to address these issues and fully embrace the grace of my journey. I have to be willing to blossom from what I thought would break me into the version of me that God sees, and I believe YOU can too. I can only hope that reading this story will help you discover your inner warrior. After all, your testimony may be the key to someone else's freedom.

It was April of 2017, and I was a senior in high school. I relocated to Louisiana from Texas a few years prior, and I was finally in a good place, mentally and spiritually. I was stuck at my grandmother's house this particular day, upset because I had been missing school too often. I did not have a car, and her house was too far from the school. Desperate to graduate, I started asking around for a ride home. I messaged everyone I knew, but no one was available. I just broke down. I had not worked so hard just to fail. My only choice was to ask *him*. He responded and said he could come. I told my grandmother that I found a ride and hugged her as I left. When he arrived, I spoke and got in on the passenger side. After so much crying, I just wanted to rest. Honestly, I was not paying attention to where he was going because I was texting my mother.

When I looked up, he had parked in a deserted field with grass that nearly covered the windows. Inside, I began to panic, so I focused on texting my mother. She knew how far my house was from my grandmother's, so she asked if I made it home safely. After not responding to multiple texts, I said yes. I lied. I should have been home, but I did not want her to worry like I was at that moment. Plus, she knew who I was with, and his life would have been in danger. After my screen locked, I noticed that my messages could be seen in the reflection of the window, and he read that my mother was going to bed. Then, the panic really set in. My thoughts were everywhere, but I tried to stay calm.

What am I going to do now? I just want to go home. Please, God, just get me home. My thoughts were interrupted when I heard him lock the doors. I glanced at him and was met with a sinister smile as he looked me up and down. At this point, I was holding back tears. I knew I was not going anywhere until he got what he wanted. I assured him that I had people waiting up for me, but to no avail. He kissed me with thin lips and heavy breathing, suggesting I was not his first victim of the night. He forcefully exposed my breasts and managed to slip his hand into my underwear as I begged him to stop. He made sure to tell me I was "so wet" as he grinned. Repeatedly and helplessly, I screamed NO, but he slid my pants to my ankles and pinned me down. I knew he was stronger than me, but this was my virginity he wanted, my body he was violating. I could not just let him win, so I resisted.

I lost track of time, dropped my phone, and was completely trapped under him when he exposed his penis from his grey shorts. His white hoodie was covered in my brown foundation, proof of my determination to make him stop. He had the look of an animal capturing its prey as I struggled. My body was positioned to where my feet were near the steering wheel. I was hysterical, so I kicked him. I was wearing black flats, but I kicked until he let me go. My vision was blurry, and my head ached. I did not know what to do, and I was shaking uncontrollably. He threw my shoe over to me, and I put it back on. He put his glasses back on, his penis back in his shorts, and sat still, watching me.

I held my head in my hands and sobbed. He sighed, shook his head, and started the car. When he got to the house, he parked the car, and I grabbed my backpack from the backseat before going inside. I held it together until I got to the bathroom and started the shower. As I undressed, I winced, touching the bruises he left on my body. I scrubbed violently, hoping to erase the filth of what had happened. *Why would God let this happen? He did not, but He did. Why couldn't someone else be available? Why?* I had so many questions, but I knew that God loved me, even if I did not feel it then.

Now, you might be wondering why I am reliving this story now. *I* never made a police report; *I* texted him for a ride. *I* responded to his text the day after. No one made me do those things, and I buried the guilt until I could deal with it. I lost myself. If you are reading this, do what I could not. Tell what happened, when, and who did it. **Do not submit to the control of your abuser by staying silent on how they hurt you**. Do not ever give someone that power over you. We are strong and powerful when we demand to be heard, so share your story. Tell someone. Free yourself, my friend. I pray that I just did.

 Aariyana Green-Smith is a published author, itinerant minister, Lupus advocate, mentor, entrepreneur, and humble servant. She is currently pursuing her master's degree in Marriage and Family Therapy at NCU.

Her business, *Privileged and Purposed LLC*, was founded in May 2020 and is a multipurpose company that offers books, branding, and so much more! Her first publication, *Phenomenal Faith*, was released in November 2019 and chronicles her battle with Lupus, an autoimmune condition that she was diagnosed with in May 2010.

This journey encouraged her to birth her travel ministry, *Spirit Unleashed Ministries*, in September 2018 to share her love of God with everyone she comes into contact with. Aariyana believes in embracing the full pursuit of an authentic relationship with Jesus Christ. She and her husband, Gabriel, currently reside in Shreveport, Louisiana, where they both teach, train, and help families acquire skills that create generational wealth and lasting financial freedom.

• CHAPTER 7 •

The Pieces of My Heart

The sounds from the machines were deafening. It was so cold in the room. I wondered if she felt it, too. Did she know I was there? The minute I walked in the room and saw her hooked up to a ventilator, I felt a piercing in my heart. I had talked to her a few hours ago, and there was no indication that she was this sick. I prayed and pleaded with God the whole way there. I had no idea it was this bad, or maybe I did. I certainly didn't expect what I saw when I walked into that room. This isn't how it happens on TV.

You pray, you cry, and they wake up. I agonized over what was going to be God's answer to my prayer. Had MY prayer not been fervent enough or passionate enough? Had I given up too soon, or was I refusing to accept the inevitable? Did I pray the right prayer? Had I been faithful and obedient enough, in my faith walk, for Him to answer MY prayers? I wondered if HE even heard my prayers; after all, I haven't always lived right. I wondered if her prayer matched my prayer. Was HE going to answer HER prayer? Had she been faithful enough for Him to answer HER prayer?

Shoot, I didn't even know what her prayer was. Maybe that was it; her prayer was not my prayer. Was I trying to hold on, and she was trying to let go? She had been near death many times before, yet it was this very routine knee replacement surgery that had her here. Less than two weeks after the surgery, here she was, DYING. It was so confusing. This time she seemed more tired than she had before. It seemed like she had made peace with whatever God had decided. She was done FIGHTING! I believe in people dying on their terms, except she didn't tell us what to do. She didn't leave a living will or a healthcare directive. She didn't discuss what we should do in this situation.

So there we were, faced with the decision to remove her from the ventilator. For the first time in my life, I had no plan. I had no answers. I had no idea what to do. I understood why she didn't fight. I understood why she was accepting of THIS being the time. I just wish she had told us what to do; and she didn't make us decide for her. If I am honest with myself, I question the decision to discontinue life support every single day. Should we have waited one more day? Did we act too soon? Would one more day have made a difference? That decision haunts me. Some days it weighs on me like a thick, heavy coat on a hot summer day. It burns my skin and penetrates my soul.

As a scientist and an educated woman, I knew what had to happen as a woman of God. As a DAUGHTER, it all just seemed so unfair. In my mind, I wanted to believe that God would bring her out. Then I remembered that I had prayed for a complete restoration. I even had the nerve to say that I understood that restoration didn't have to happen on this side, but either way it turned out she would be restored. The problem is that in grief, the heart and the mind are seldom on one accord. My mind agreed, but my heart didn't have it. My heart wondered why death couldn't knock at someone else's door.

The educated woman in me understood that she was tired. The DAUGHTER in me was just so heartbroken. The DAUGHTER in me needed just one MORE day, one more laugh, one more hug, one more "I Love You." The DAUGHTER in me said, "Couldn't you have picked ANOTHER time, not December?" The follower of Christ in me understood why He chose December. In the month that celebrated HIS birth, HE decided that HIS daughter had suffered ENOUGH. HE decided that what better time to give her a RE-BIRTH than in the month that celebrates HIS birth. I wasn't testing God, but I sure was questioning God.

I felt like mommy got the short end of the stick when she was stuck with me to help her make that journey. I mean, everybody knows that I am not **THAT** daughter. I am not the "nurse you back to health" daughter. Our entire lives, it was my sister that has been the ONE. She had been the caretaker for everyone. I volunteered to stay, only because I thought that my sister wouldn't let me, or she would stay too. I couldn't be trusted with this monumental task. But mommy was stuck with ME, the one who was NOT THAT daughter. I'm sure she wondered how she ended up with me in her final hours. I now understand that I NEEDED to be there. There was an assignment that I had to complete.

You are never prepared for a loss this great. Even when you know it's coming, it is earth-shattering. When her heart stopped beating, so did mine. When she stopped breathing, so did I. When she died, so did I. Many told me it was a blessing to be with my mother when she transitioned, but it didn't feel like one. It was of no comfort to me to imagine life WITHOUT her and see the life leaving her body. However, I am eternally grateful that I was FORCED to become THAT daughter. I am glad that God knew I needed to hold her hand until the end. That journey made me a better mother, sister, and friend. There is no time frame associated with grief. You can't ignore it. You can't wish it away, cry it away, or drink it away. Just like any other deep wound, you need to have a wound care treatment plan to heal.

Mommy, I'm healing ♡

Dr. Sonya Strider is a Public Health professional and a certified Grief Recovery Method Specialist with the Grief Recovery Institute. After losing both parents within nine months, Sonya found herself wading through the muddy waters of insurmountable grief.

Searching for ways to deal with her grief, she discovered the Grief Recovery Institute and the Grief Recovery Method. Sonya helps grievers heal from life losses, including death, divorce, relationships, jobs, and more. Through healing and recovery, she strives to help grievers do the work to complete their grieving and find hope and joy again.

Contact:
https://www.griefrecoverymethod.com/grms/sonya-strider

• CHAPTER 8 •

Real Love (Unconditionally)

I am my momma's only child. Dad passed away when I was seven, and mom remarried. I gained a hardcore stepdad from Broward County and two siblings who were raised completely different from me. My upbringing was a lot less innovative or exciting than theirs. Then crack cocaine hit our community and made its way into our home. This was an introduction to the lifestyle and situations I had heard my siblings talk about.

Everything changed as I was preparing to leave for college—timing was terrible. While mom worked two-sometimes-three shifts as a nursing assistant to provide for me, I was running into housing projects looking for my stepdad and our car for transportation. So often, I found the car in the middle of the night and took it. It was almost a routine to find our car in crack-infested locations. I became the responsible one at an early age. I took mom to and from work, driving myself to school, and attending daily dance rehearsals for competitions. No one knew what was going on except the young drug dealers who told me where I could find my stepdad. Mom worked so many hours - overnight and double shifts to pay the mortgage and take care of me. Other caring parents helped me the most during times when mom wasn't available.

FAMU, here I come!

I never felt more fortunate about attending Florida Agriculture and Mechanical University. Tallahassee bound was all that was in my purview. It was a great way to make a fresh start, but there was one issue. The only way I could attend FAMU was to find housing off-campus as a freshman since all dormitories were booked. Due to the everyday events back home, mom told me I was now an adult who she knows could handle what was to come and not mess this up—talk about "pressure." I immediately thought about how I would find transportation to and from campus.

The day I arrived in Tallahassee I was so nervous. It was 6 am, and my mom made it clear, it was a day to find an apartment, bed, and necessities because she had to be back in Daytona for work at 11 pm. It seemed so wrong to be dropped off at eighteen in a new city and apartment with $500 to get me started. By this time, we had lost our home due to my stepdad's drug dependency, and mom worked all the shifts she could to help me.

Learning to Believe

After college, I moved to Northern Virginia with a lifelong girlfriend to pursue better opportunities in my field (Public Relations). I slept on her apartment floor for months. There was one important goal–finding a church home. When I found my church home, I found a roommate/landlord too. It wasn't ideal for a young lady because he was a male in his late thirties–at least fifteen years, my senior. I spoke to my mom about the arrangement; we prayed on it, and she called me the next day saying the Holy Spirit spoke to her, saying I should take advantage of the opportunity and something good will come from me trusting God.

I moved in, found temporary work at a Public Relations firm, but had an odd exchange with a Caucasian woman. I was terminated and devastated. My roommate introduced me to his fiancé, who got me a job at Freddie Mac. This was a career move that lasted eight years. But with stiff competition, a new city, an environment with unfamiliar faces, not much money or food, and frequent layoffs – all of this made it extremely hard to focus and be happy. I was often afraid and unsure. Returning home wasn't an option because Mom said "No, you gotta keep pushing." For years to come, finding stability was a struggle.

Finally . . . New Life, New Wife, and Stepmom (I should be happy)

While many close friends lived their lives with husbands, babies, and beautiful homes, I was still single and dealing with heartaches and bad experiences. I felt slighted, alone, and sad all the time. But years later, an old friend found me and never let go. The situation was not ideal, but the sincerity and consistency he showed me were refreshing. He was hundreds of miles away and divorced with three kids. We both had insecurities and baggage that did not help our situation at all. We committed to seeing each other twice a month until we found ourselves together as one. It was hard and expensive. After spending so much time and money on flights, rental cars, and hotel vacationing, it was time to decide to relocate.

I moved to Georgia, and the real work began. I was adjusting to change well. My priority was about the "mister" and a career. But I was fooling myself because I really wanted to be married. I had made the biggest sacrifice of my life, moving to be with a man and not married. I began to question the depth of our relationship because I wanted things to happen in my timing. I felt guilt every time things got difficult or uncomfortable. Then, outside drama entered my life. A few friends made their feelings known about my move and my man. Negative things were said behind my back and to others. I felt betrayed and embarrassed.

He proposed and I accepted. Marrying at forty-five wasn't ideal, but it was happening. Lies, jealousy, and deceit were upon us. Lots of negative talk and gossip occurred. There's an old saying that says the devil shows up real big at weddings and funerals. Well, he didn't stop the progress of a beautiful foundation. I prayed for strength and stability daily. No one knew the depth of such pain. The lesson I learned is to be careful about what you share. Your happiness is not for others, it is for you.

Ruth Dixon-Taylor is a federal contractor with over fifteen years of IT experience and business owner/creator of *Naturally Taylor'd*™ *Skin*, a new cosmetics company specializing in handmade natural lotions and products for all skin types. She is a graduate of Florida A&M University and a Journalism major from Daytona Beach.

She lived in the DC, MD, and VA (DMV) area for eighteen years before relocating and settling down in Atlanta (2015) to get married for the first time at age forty-five. Ruth is loved and adored by her husband and three wonderful sons. Ruth's life hasn't been all peaches and cream, which is why she jumped on the opportunity to collaborate with her fellow co-authors to share her life's experiences. She is confident that God presented this platform to share her experiences with others. Ruth embraces her calling to inspire others to believe.

• CHAPTER 9 •

Overcoming a Loyalty of Lies

"You ain't nothing, and you'll never be nothing! And nobody will ever want you with all those children!" When I heard these words from the one I tried to love, I knew our family reached a point of no return. I began to question how could one spew so much hate towards the family they say they love? Is it possible to love again after hearing such harsh comments made towards children who looked up to their parents as everything?

As a mother, you always want the best for your children and never want to see them in the space of hurt and pain. But on this day, I felt so broken, so helpless, so distraught. This day not only was filled with much pain of witnessing children you birthed become lifeless, but I also experienced having to say goodbye as two of my four daughters decided they could not take anymore. They packed all their belongings and left. Never to return to live in the home where they were raised. In this home, we celebrated many milestones, the home where I cooked their favorite meals, the home where we celebrated holidays and birthdays. In this home, we comforted each other during seasons of family sickness and death.

I then had to come to terms and realize I had seen the signs of a family breakdown for years, but for the first time, I could no longer think, "How can we fix this?" but this question now turned to, "How much longer can we go on?" As women we sacrifice so much for our families, but are we ever appreciated? Are we appreciated for cooking the meals but always being the last to eat? Are we appreciated for picking up and dropping off without a "thank you?" Are we appreciated for being our spouse's maid, secretary, cook, and sexual partner when they desire?

In my case, the answer was no. I realized I truly was being treated as less than when I struggled to work sixteen-hour days in my business for the sake of my family, to keep us on board financially. When I received the phone call, I remember that it was already decided to purchase a brand-new Cadillac. However, I served as the taxi driver for the children with a broken air conditioner, tires with no tread, and many mechanical problems. I was once again reminded of "How much longer can we go on?" Many may read this and say, "Is that it? Is this all you have to complain about?" But the answer is NOT!

There were many instances of hurt and pain over the years, but I realized when a family demise is occurring, the final moments are imprinted in your mind. The constant mental abuse, arguing, lying, infidelities were the villain in multiple situations. Having to be the fall guy for every situation that went wrong, in addition to the daily sacrifice and hard work of raising a family, the hands holding on were slowly losing grip. I knew my family was in a lot of trouble when I could answer yes to all the following questions:

1. **Does your partner frequently seem irritated or angry with you, although you never meant to upset them?**
2. **Do you feel confused by their raging anger?**
3. **Have you frequently felt perplexed and frustrated by your partner's responses because you can't get them to understand your intentions?**

4. **Has your partner been jealous or possessive of you?**
5. **Have you been accused of having affairs or paying too much attention to others?**
6. **Does your partner make you feel like you are mostly wrong, and they are always right?**

At that moment, I felt a lot of mixed emotions. I was relieved in realizing I was not crazy and what I was dealing with was an apparent narcissistic behavior. I was despondent because I realized there was nothing that I could do to help this situation. The bottom line was narcissistic tendencies can improve with support from a trained therapist. I knew this was a lost cause because first, the narcissist must recognize a problem, take responsibility for the issues, and re-prioritize what is important. This would not happen, which ultimately was the cause and the complete catastrophic collapse of our family.

As usual, I have always been deemed as the problem. I had to decide between rescuing myself and my children to live a good life, and finally be free and happy. As soon as I decided a way was made, and the universe started moving things for me to have what I put out in the atmosphere, but believe me, the narcissist made sure every step I took towards freedom would come with a price. The people I needed to help me with this transition arrived. The doors I needed to open were unblocked but lurking behind the door of freedom was a hell I never thought I would ever have to experience, especially after living such a life constantly living on pins and needles.

The deceptive plots and plans laid for me were carefully calculated with a team of earthly demonic imps that helped carry out the plans. The day I was made aware that these imps were from my own family, friends who knew me since childhood, and church members I thought loved me like family, my heart felt pains I never knew possible. This was the day I realized people really can die from a broken heart.

Look out for the continuation of this painful plan and how it unfolded by nearly paralyzing me emotionally, physically, and financially for three years. Learn how it took every ounce of my being to crawl back into existence. You won't believe the created plots put into motion to destroy me. To be continued…

Dr. Sherry Adams is the Tri-State Luxury Group owner serving Georgia, Florida, and Alabama and has multiple national designations/certifications. She joined Century 21 in 2001 and quickly rose to General Managing Broker, managing 200+ Agents.

She is a 25+ year national and international award-winning educator. Dr. Adams received her bachelor's degree from Clark College, master's and doctorate degree from Clark Atlanta University, graduating with a 3.95 GPA. She also received an associate degree from Genesis School of Ministry.

Dr. Adams is a member of Delta Sigma Theta Sorority, Inc. and is a National Board-Certified Teacher. She served on the National Board of Professional Teaching Standards and Board of Directors chaired by former Georgia Governor Roy Barnes. Sherry and her mother also founded the Miss Black Teen Atlanta Scholarship Pageant at the Georgia World Congress Center for 10+ years, where over $175,000 in scholarships were awarded.

• CHAPTER 10 •

It's Time...

She looked so graceful; my friend, at her husband's wake, as she grieved his untimely passing. He suddenly died while they were getting ready for work and school, leaving her devastated. Her usual warm, engaging smile was tired and partial. Her eyes were low, unrested, and drifting; it was sad, beautiful, vulnerable, and strong all at the same moment. She was the picture of a grieving widow. And that's when it hit me... It was time to leave my abusive ten-year marriage.

I imagined how I'd feel in her shoes. I'm not as graceful as my beautifully mourning friend. I have no poker face, and I'm not an effective liar. My inappropriate joy and relief would likely have gotten me investigated or at least gossiped about for years. I wished my husband would just disappear and relieve me of him, his family, and his abuse.

Also, I felt I deserved the benefits due to his family. I wanted to get all dressed up with my family and friends and say a final goodbye to him, but it wouldn't be sad. We wouldn't wear black. It would be a colorful party with decorations, drinks, lively music, dancing, and smiles, in a funeral home, not my house. That's what my husband's wake would look like if it happened that day. And I knew that was a problem.

At times during our ten-year marriage, I thought we would make it. I thought we would grow together and conquer our marital toxicity. I now realize I was expecting him to change. "When I can get him to (fill in the blank), we'll be fine." In those blanks was: be nice, stop yelling, save money, pay bills, relax, talk to me, help with the kids, tell the truth, stop holding grudges… None of that was ever going to happen. When we first met, his passion and power with people amazed me. It was beautiful and fascinating to see how people seemed to respect him. He was also very attentive. He was interested in whatever I was doing, talking about, or interested in. It seemed like adoration and compatibility. Everywhere I went, he went. Whoever I spoke with, he spoke with. I was committed to our marriage and family, but I desperately needed some space for myself.

I learned it was insecurity and machismo where gentle masculinity should have been, that drove his controlling and possessive behaviors. He started to feel more like a dependent than a partner, and my attraction to him waned. When our intimacy vanished, resentment and frustration took its place and grew like weeds. Soon after the birth of our third child, our marriage snapped.

I sought professional help to understand how I tolerated his abuse. First, the abuse was mostly verbal, which can be dismissed as just "fussing." I'm here to tell you that's bullshit. When a person is yelling, cursing, and complaining continuously, it wears down your spirit, disrupts your peace, hardens your heart, and I'm sure more than that. That's just what it did to me! It made me pretend to sleep-in some mornings, work late, take on extra projects, and avoid phone calls (mostly his). It placed nervous energy in my home that wouldn't allow me to relax or creatively express myself. It made me feel unsafe and very unhappy.

Counseling also helped me recognize that my family, who I love very much and am super proud of, is very disrespectful. They didn't know it. My parents were great, and I can't speak poorly of them as mentors, role models, or parents. They weren't perfect and had weak points, but I have more gratitude for them than criticisms. However, with fourteen siblings between them, all of whom were very close to us, who we interacted with nearly daily, my family felt wonderfully huge and magnificently flawed. They diluted some of my parent's views, and respect fell into that.

Consequently, I didn't recognize disrespect, so I didn't effectively address it, if at all. And when I say disrespectful, I mean little things like always coming to events late. Respect others' time! Making jokes at another person's expense is disrespectful and cruel. It's not funny to laugh about a person's mistakes, flaws, or vulnerabilities in group settings. Being casual with another person's belongings is disrespectful. Example: if I say stay out of my room, don't go in there, and then tell me it was only for a minute. You just disrespected my wishes and my room. When you add it all up, disrespectful behavior was my way of life.

This also means that I was pretty good at being disrespectful, but I didn't know it. I thought I was being free and honest. I didn't yell a lot, so if I'm calm, I can't be disrespectful, right? Wrong!! I can disrespect you so quick you'll wonder how I did it, but now, it's only intentional. I used to do it subconsciously. I was so comfortable with disrespect that I let it in the door and found it a seat. Please don't come for me unless you're ready for battle with your first aid kit, was my thinking.

I challenged my husband's upbringing under the guise of honesty, but I didn't consider his family dynamic or feelings. I insulted him, abused his trust and spirit with my words. I held my own in our abusive marriage. The difference between us was that being a parent was changing me, but not us. I was tired and longed for something different, so we went to our last of three marriage counselors. Counseling showed me that I dated, married, and built a life with a man who didn't love me, and who I likely didn't love. Our pain drew and kept us together because it recognized itself in each of our souls. We were from two entirely different backgrounds, single mother vs. dual parents, New York immigrants vs. Southerners, uneducated vs. highly educated, physical abuse, and disrespect. There were differences, yet the pain was the same.

Yep, it was time.

 Keeva Linton is a self-supporting divorced mother of three. She has overcome depression, financial abandonment, domestic abuse, and homelessness. She is also very involved in her community, launching and leading Westlake High School Alumni Association.

Co-creating with some of her classmates in a sports summer camp that employed local students, launching a recycling company, holding executive offices within school organizations, and contributing to her school system's diversity efforts. Currently, this author works in Information Technology in healthcare as a consultant to healthcare organizations and hospitals around the country. She is a proud graduate of Clark Atlanta University and a member of their Athletic Hall of Fame.

Keeva lives with her three children, Vance, Reese, and Chase, and dog Luna in the northwest suburbs of Atlanta, Georgia.

• CHAPTER 11 •

Embracing My Ausome World

Friday, September 6, 2013, started like any other day in my pregnancy. I was happy, yet tired, swollen, sleepy, and experiencing weird cravings while headed to my monthly maternal fetal medicine visit. I was 35-years old when I conceived my daughter, so I was automatically considered a high-risk pregnancy. My husband and I had prayed for her and "planned" her, so we knew that this pregnancy was God ordained; and that my age or being high risk was nothing for God and us to handle.

As I sat in the back waiting for the doctor, the medical assistant came to take my blood pressure. After about 5 different attempts with different blood pressure cuffs, the MA went to get the nurse and doctor. The doctor came in and immediately put her fingers up in front of me and asked how many fingers did I see? Was my vision blurred? Did I have a headache? She told me that my blood pressure as dangerously high and she was calling the ambulance to take me to hospital immediately. I agreed to drive myself to the hospital since it was only a 5-minute drive. Within an hour of arriving, I was being told that I was going to be induced and that I was going to have a baby. I was told that I had developed pre-eclampsia. Pre-eclampsia is a dangerous pregnancy complication triggered by high blood pressure and can be fatal for the mother and child.

I'd planned my life and pregnancy; and so far, life was happening as *I* desired up until that point. I spent the next 60 hours in labor with the medical team attempting to get my little girl to come on her own. Suddenly, at 1:17 a.m. on September 9, 2013 I heard a nurse rush into my room and tell my husband to put on scrubs, we were about to have a baby. The next thing I remembered was sitting up, falling over, and waking up 18 hours later.

When I woke up, I was groggy but excited and wanted to see and hold my baby. I was taken to the Neonatal Intensive Care Unit (NICU) where I saw my 3-pound 1-ounce baby covered in tubes and struggling to breathe. The next day she lost 10 ounces and the doctors became nervous. My husband and I prayed, and God did what He always does. Camille began to gain weight, thrive, and develop as any typical baby, and left the NICU after three weeks.

Year one for Camille was nothing short of amazing. She hit all milestones ahead of time for her growth and development. She did what any other child her age would have been doing during their first year. In year two we began to observe that Camille had exceptional speed and was very calculating in her play. We also noticed she was becoming withdrawn and no longer using her words. We contacted a pediatrician who told us not to worry, some kids talk later.

A couple months went by and her second birthday was approaching. We planned a party with her favorite cartoon character at the time and invited kids from her daycare. Camille was withdrawn and clung to her dad the entire time. She cried non-stop and just seemed overwhelmed. We thought maybe she wasn't feeling well, but we knew something else was going on. I begin to Google some of the behaviors and the regressed speech, and repeatedly saw AUTISM; my heart sank. I scheduled her for an examination with a pediatric psychologist and was initially told after the examination that she did not have enough symptoms and that she should reevaluated when she turns three.

I was not satisfied with that and found another doctor to evaluate Camille. This time we got the dreaded diagnosis of Autism Spectrum Disorder with speech delay and Sensory Processing Disorder. I sat and cried in the doctor's office and my husband held me and told me that Camille would be just fine. I immediately thought of all the things that I had read about Autism and all the limitations that so many people with ASD experience. The things that most children her age were doing she was either not interested, or unable to do them. While my daughter had exceptional speed and could tumble with precision better than kids older than her, I grieved that I had to withdraw my daughter from gymnastics because she could not follow instructions.

Washing her hair was a daunting 2-hour task that me and my husband dreaded. I cried because I couldn't put ponytails and barrettes in her hair like other little girls because they irritated her. The life that I'd imagined for my daughter seemed as if it would never be. As Camille grows, I've accepted what I perceived as challenges or delays simply as differences. My grief has shifted to praise and thanksgiving.

I've come to see that Camille can do what most children can do, just differently. She is the smartest, most observant and discerning little girl that I have ever encountered. I realized that Camille's autism diagnosis is not punishment nor is it about me or Camille. As always, God has a greater plan for our experiences. The blessing in my child having autism will help so many other families gain support and resources about autism. I've started a foundation, The Ausome World, to support organizations that provide respite care for parents of autistic children.

Today, Camille still doesn't like to get her hair done, but she likes the finished products of ponytails. She is a seven-year-old techy, has several hundred words in her vocabulary, but says them when she wants to. She loves to sing nursery rhymes as she watches them on her tablet. I would say that she is pretty AUSOME! While Camille may have some delays now, I'm confident that she will lead a normal life, and we will continue to embrace our AUSOME world.

Carla Moultrie is the second oldest child of six children to the late Mr. Freddie Jordan and the late Mrs. Carrie Jordan. She is a native of Florida's sunshine state and proud alumni of Florida Agricultural and Mechanical University; she gave her life to her Lord and Savior, Jesus Christ, in the summer of 1998. She has served as children's Sunday school teacher, choir director, and women's group leader.

Professionally, she has over 17 years of contract management experience and has worked for the Florida Supreme Court and several major corporations. She is currently studying to sit for the Law School Admissions Test (LSAT). For almost 12 years, she has shared her life with her husband, Pastor Nathaniel Moultrie, and together they have two daughters Moriah and Camille.

She is passionate about encouraging and empowering women and children. She believes that she is divinely called to advocate for families navigating Autism and helping children embrace children different from them. She plans to advocate for families navigating autism through her non-profit, *The Ausome World*, and engage other children through her organization, *Ausome Girl*.

• CHAPTER 12 •

Looking Ahead

"I've decided that I don't want to be married anymore."

All these years later, I can still remember how it felt when his words took shape in my brain, and the raw pain that pierced my heart and took my breath away. We were a young military couple, married less than three years and straight off a year of living apart because of his solo tour of duty. I had just moved into base housing and was newly unemployed. I was settling into the thought of playing housewife for a while. As it turned out, he had met someone less than a month before the "grand announcement."

A few days later, I was lying across the bed, not feeling well, when the house phone rang. As he picked up the living room, I picked up the bedroom phone. I heard an unfamiliar voice addressing him with familiarity. To my surprise, he responded excitedly. I immediately spoke up, "What's going on? Who is this?" That is how I found out that my husband was leaving me for another woman.

I was so sick, so hurt, so angry, such a ball of beat down emotion that I could not move. I couldn't keep food down. I was lightheaded and dizzy. One afternoon, still lying in the bed that I had not left for nearly a week, the phone rang as it had been almost non-stop for the past few days. This time, he was there to answer. He came to the bedroom door and said, "Cindy is on the phone. She says that if you don't talk to her, she's going to drive five hours to see what's going on with you." I took the phone.

"I've been calling you for the last three days. Girl, what is going on with you?"

"He's leaving me for someone else."

Cindy was speechless for a full minute. Her responses and questions began falling from her mouth in a rapid staccato of words, phrases, and unfinished sentences. Her disbelief became acute in its completeness.

"Y'all were just laughing and happy. What happened?"

"I have no idea. All I know is that I haven't been able to eat. I can't keep anything down, and I've been sick since he told me."

"That sounds like more than heartbreak. I think you should go to the doctor."

At sick call the next day, the pregnancy test result was positive. I understood that I was facing being the one thing that I never wanted to be - an unemployed, single mother. When I told Kyle my not-so-happy news, I thought a sense of honor and duty, or even responsibility to this life inside me would change his mind. When I showed him the test results, his first words were, "I guess I will have to tell her so we can figure this out." Foolishly, I thought his next words would have been an apology. I thought that what we would be figuring out was how to stay married.

Instead, he said, "I'm going to be moving next week. She and I are getting a place. I've informed the housing office. You will have thirty days to move. You can have all the furniture. She has some." I felt like Bernadette in "Waiting to Exhale" when John told her he was leaving. Oh, if only I'd had the gumption to set something on fire. The next few weeks would see him calling to have my car picked up by the finance company. I would come home to find him and her sitting on our couch, wanting to discuss how we would co-parent the lime-sized, thirteen-week-old fetus still growing in my stomach. I invited them to leave while holding an eight-inch hunting knife.

All the while, the deadline to vacate base housing loomed near. I had no job, no car, no money, and all-day sickness, still unable to keep anything down. I even ended up in the emergency room dehydrated and as it turned out, already needing a procedure to save the baby. Afterwards, I was immediately ordered to complete bed rest. Initially, my pride would let me only tell Cindy; not my parents or any of my other friends. I would just lie in bed, trying to figure out what it was I had done to deserve this.

With less than two weeks to eviction, I finally reached out to my parents. My stepmom became one half of the spirit team that would be my guardian angels through the process. The other half of my team was Dee, a former co-worker, and his wife. They were and still are the best people. My stepmom wired $400 that I used to rent a Ryder truck. Dee came to my house one Saturday morning and nearly alone, loaded up the truck with our meager furniture. I helped as much as I could, temporarily ignoring the bedrest orders.

Monday morning, less than a week before being evicted, I hopped into the driver's seat of that big yellow truck. I made only one stop on the way out of town--the garage on base where my estranged husband worked. I wanted to give him one more chance to ask, to plead, to beg me to stay. I promised him that once I turned the corner in that truck, that I would have to leave any hope for us behind. I even told him about all the times that my grandmother told me the story of Lot's wife. Reminding me not to look back, only look forward. He firmly bid me farewell, seemingly without a hint of compassion, care, or concern about me, or our unborn child that was just starting to round out my belly. I climbed back into the cab, turned the ignition, and headed down the road, looking ahead to the next chapter.

Cee Mitchell is your self-appointed Ambassador of Goodness and Light, your assistant Life Coach, your biggest cheerleader, and most importantly, your spiritual fitness advocate. She knows a thing or two about energy flow and the importance of regularly sitting with yourself in silence in her meditation coaching practice.

As to her professional credentials, she has several years of experience across several fields. For the last eight years, she has managed a customer service contract at Atlanta's airport with an annual budget of a million dollars-plus. She is an Abundance Now Ambassador, partnered with Lisa Nichols and Motivating the Masses. From time to time, she lends her voice and leadership skills as a conference facilitator. She writes one-page resumes for those entering the job market for the first time and is an interview coach.

Sometimes, if she really likes you, she will take on the occasional role as a Day of Wedding Coordinator. She has a passion for doodling, photography as a hobby/business, and taking naps in her downtime. She enjoys cooking healthy meals for her husband, Marcus, aka M, aka

TGHE (The Greatest Husband Ever), and walking *his* dog, GiGi. Their favorite thing to do together is to hang out in their "couple's cave" that they have named the "Two Suns Music Room."

• CHAPTER 13 •

Will You Abort, Miscarry, or Birth

The affirmation and love that a little girl gets from her daddy were foreign to me. I saw others with their fathers, but I could not make the connection. Dad was absent. He caused heartache, anger, and pain. I later realized the outpouring I needed from him, and the generational curses would affect my life in ways I could not imagine. Although our story is one of reconciliation and forgiveness, I am working through self-love and finding out the impact of my decisions on my journey.

Abort

The lack of a father-figure directly impacted my self-worth, romantic relationships, and emotional attachments. Sex became a way of expression. It felt good to release. I felt something that appeared to be love and the connection that left a constant longing. My promiscuity led to the fulfillment of the scripture to "be fruitful and multiply." However, I stopped there. I did not dare to follow through. I cut life short too many times to keep myself going through the painful journey that would expose my secret indiscretions' shame. That immediate gratification caused lasting pains that I still deal with today.

What is it that you have aborted? Was it God's plan, or was the abortion an act of fear because you didn't trust God? Have you had multiple abortions due to stagnation with fear, which caused a vicious cycle of promiscuity with your dreams because you have been desensitized of your harmful ways? Have you become a dream killer?

Miscarry

I knew there was a problem before I even made it to the doctor. The signs of life had escaped me, and there was nothing I could do. We hadn't been married a year, and it was already on the rocks. Then the big news... The amazing part is that I had two other people in my family pregnant at the same time. They made their announcement; I followed suit but never made it full term. I lost what I believed to have been my most desired son before making it through the first trimester. As I watch their children develop through the milestones of life, I wonder what could have been. Tears flow, pain emerges, and memories flood my mind until I melt into the floor and ask, "God, why my baby?"

Maybe you have not physically lost a child, but you have lost sight of your dream/assignment/purpose/calling. What have you carried as an earnest desire? You've thought about it for months or maybe even years. You told God when He blessed you to bring it to life; you'd honor Him with it. Then something happened. You may or may not be able to put your finger on the exact date, but if you think hard enough, you can remember when the feeling was gone.

Did you share it prematurely with someone else? You thought just maybe you could walk the journey together, but God said not so. You lost yours, and s/he carried out the plan successfully. Not only have you lost your way, but their success constantly reminds you of what you feel you should've had. Did you leave God out of the plan? Was it too soon? Did you get off course watching someone else's timeline? What happened? You miscarried your dream/assignment.

I was mad at God and couldn't understand. I finally did it the right way, and it was all crumbling right before my eyes. The last glimpse of hope was life snatched away from me. To add insult to injury, I had to carry that dead fetus for a week before he was taken. I still had the signs of life, though. The morning sickness and cravings were there. My desire to talk to him was there. What did I do wrong? How could I have saved my unborn child? What regrets are tied to your miscarried assignment? You think you've done everything right, but God still allowed death to occur. What are you asking God about what you have miscarried?

Full-Term

The nine months of carrying were vastly different from both pregnancies. I was stretched beyond what I felt my small frame could handle, and it was painfully uncomfortable. The joy of December 9, 1999, and November 14, 2008, replaced the pain I had just experienced days before. The completion of the birthing process left me overwhelmed yet fulfilled.

I had an emergency cesarean with my second daughter. Although we discussed this as an option due to her expected birth weight, I was determined to have her naturally like my first daughter. It happened totally different than I planned. Ironically, I never wanted children and thought I would live my life selfishly doing what I wanted to do. God saw differently and blessed me with two amazing daughters. I believe they were used to save me from myself. The requirement to become an adult and accept responsibility was immediate. I had to think about my steps carefully because it was about someone beyond me. What is inside of you that God is trying to push out? Are you pliable and allowing Him to do it the way He wants?

Birthing Plan: Nuggets for a successful birthing experience

The "baby" inside of you is depending on you to birth it. Beware of distractions. Be vigilant about protecting your peace. There will be attacks from every side, so you must be careful to walk in wisdom. Be careful of your diet, including what you watch, eat, and who consumes your time. Your surroundings and your support team will be crucial to ensure you are protecting yourself during this season. Capture your moments through journaling and rely on God as your guide. While it may not manifest how you felt it would, He has your best interest and will do more than we can ever ask or think. The birthing process may not be easy, but it will be worth it, so write the vision and make it plain.

Sabrina Pressley lives in the metro Atlanta area with her exceptionally perfect daughters and dog. In addition to beginning this adventure as an author, Sabrina is a school administrator in one of the largest metro area school districts. She has poured twenty years into her career. Ms. Pressley is a goal-driven, resourceful and dedicated educator committed to developing each child in her care socially and academically.

Her commitment to creating a school environment that is encouraging yet stimulating to children is evident. She is devoted to developing her staff and students by being an example of professional ethics, standing on the standards of practice, and caring for all people. She remains motivated through daily reflective introspection and encouraging others through her actions to maximize their potential.

• CHAPTER 14 •

Who Cares for the Caregiver?

So, you really thought when I was caring for my sister, whose body was stricken with cancer, I was just gon' listen to YOU tell me what to do about MY sister? You tried it. You don't get to tell me what I should and shouldn't do or what I should've done. Don't you know I heard your whispers about what you thought her situation was? Tuh, God gifted me with bionic ears and telepathy. I heard and saw you the moment you put your mouth on her, but I chose to respond to what I wanted to. The venom of my silence is the deadliest strike you will ever feel. Wanda died from cancer complications. It was no secret, but it wasn't yo' damn business.

It was October 2008, five months after she had given birth to my nephew, when she told me about the possibility of a diagnosis. Wanda wouldn't find out for sure that she had stage four breast cancer until February 2009. It was a long wait for the second opinion. After getting results, she fainted, literally passed out. They gave Wanda smelling salts to awaken her. The news was devastating to Wanda as it was, in her mind, the beginning to an end. Not the end to her life, but to the life she knew. Her words to me were, "I'm going to do everything I have to do to live, and you have to help me."

Over the phone, she shared the news with me and in my calmness whenever I hear any news; I told my sister she was stronger than she knew. In that moment, I immediately became the baby sister who was the caregiver of an older, married sister. The middle child to a daddy who raised two girls after the death of his wife and now the youngest daughter taking on a role to a daddy that the oldest sister so proudly treasured.

A sister who had to console a brother who cherished his oldest sister with whom he shared an unbreakable bond. A full-time working mommy to a two-sport, college junior honor-student athlete daughter, who people often mistaken her auntie as her mother. An auntie (in love with her baby nephew) who would use photos, stories, memories to preserve his mother's legacy, should she pass.

A girlfriend to a guy that required attention. A sister-in-law to a brother-in-law who may be widowed, in need of support in raising a son.

A family member who would have to communicate the health status of their favorite girl because cancer had her forgetting things. A spokesperson to Wanda's classmates who wanted to know; and the regulator to those who prematurely speculated and shared inaccurate and unapproved details about MY sister on social media, private chats, and in personal discussions. Soon I became the one that many didn't want to fuck with because my response to their inquiries usually started with a side eye and ended with "Why you asking?" Especially if I knew or thought someone was disingenuous about MY sister's condition. I was that girl, and I was OVERWHELMED!

Did I tell you? Wanda was a very well-known and talented master cosmetologist in the Atlanta, College Park, and Newnan, GA areas. Her clientele was huge, consisting of children, high-schoolers, homemakers, working mothers, single women, wives of celebrities, entrepreneurs, shit starters, trash talkers, and others I didn't mention. She embraced them all. Wanda had a way of connecting with all of her clients. I remember hearing her tell her clients,

"Earrings and lipstick, please. You not walking outta here with your hair laid and your face not beat."

As her shampoo assistant, I would hear the pep talks and encouraging words she spoke to and over her clients. I identified and remembered the ones she had to get told. Even after her diagnosis, Wanda continued to do hair, eventually leaving the salon to offer mobile service because the smell of chemicals had become too much for her. I was there every step of the way, assisting her when she was too tired to drive, stand, and move, but still doing hair. After I worked 50 hours a week, I was the caregiver who would get up at 3 am on Saturday mornings to drive her to her clients' homes to shampoo their hair.

I would wait for Wanda to finish, then we would drive to another client's home to repeat the same routine. I was also the caregiver who made sure Wanda ate while working because her taste buds were all over the place, played tricks on her making her think she wanted a breakfast sandwich, but instead, it was something else I would end up getting. I was that girl...EXHAUSTED! Wanda passed on August 27, 2010, ten days before her birthday. The scenarios mentioned above were of many I experienced. But I was the strong one nobody checked on.

People misunderstood my calm demeanor, skill for organization, level head, good decision-making, and handling business as their go-to girl (even when I didn't want to be) to get things done. I was OVERWHELMED and EXHAUSTED, and it never crossed their minds that I was. I'm here to tell you, watching my sister fade away wasn't easy, along with checking stupid motherfuckers who had something to say. Checking them wasn't hard because the way I check motherfuckers is with no profanity, just an eye piercing stare, one eyebrow raised, and calm voice, remembering that I'm still a lady.

I made it through with prayer. I had to see about me and become my own caregiver. I began lighting candles, meditating, REALLY talking to God, asking for strength, and taking moments for myself daily, no matter what. Finally, I understood! God chose ME for it all and to be her caregiver. Realizing this gave me solace to approach tasks and challenges that came with caring for my beloved sister Wanda and caring for me, all at the same time.

Thank you, Jesus!

Carrie T. Hamilton-Shavers is a Doctoral Candidate at Clark Atlanta University, and the owner of *Another TUT Production, LLC*, a fashion entertainment production company, and *opporTUTnity, Inc.*, a non-profit organization focusing on education and training services.

Her background includes writing for fashion theatre, mass communications, counseling psychology, and education curriculum development for detained juveniles, training, non-profit and state government work experience, and senior citizen engagement. She is a qualified mental health professional who silently uses her skills to help others become the best version of themselves.

Hamilton-Shavers obtained a Bachelor of Arts in mass communication (radio-TV-film) and a master's in counseling psychology (community counseling) from Clark Atlanta University. She's currently a doctoral candidate in Higher Education Leadership at Clark Atlanta University and is an active member of Delta Sigma Theta Sorority, Incorporated. She speaks loudly for the caregivers because they oftentimes are not heard.

• CHAPTER 15 •

From Check Him to Check Me

The weight of him was so heavy. I don't know which was heavier, his body or the weight of the relationship. He was sitting on my waist, pinning me to the bed. It felt like my body was going to snap in two and my breathing was labored under his 400 pounds. I thought of ways to break free from his hold. I tried to break free but couldn't. He grabbed a vase from the night table. While holding it in the air, he menacingly said, "I will fuck up your face so that no man will ever want you."

I blinked my eyes, and I found myself sitting in my therapist's office. I sat on the sofa and positioned myself slightly erect while leaning forward. I started to fidget with the tissue box on the table as I am carefully pouring out my filtered heart, refusing to make eye contact. Peering over white-rimmed glasses, the therapist listened intently. I watched her stare at me, scribble, stare at me, then scribble some more. Each time she began to take notes, it was as if the sound of the pencil scratching the paper would get louder and louder.

In previous sessions, I'd completed the "Wheel of Abuse" test. Per the test, I was indeed an abuse victim in multiple areas. I'd expected her to give me another victim title from the Wheel. I had even braced myself for it. I paused, stern-faced waiting to hear her thoughts. Little did I know, that session would be different. She abruptly stopped scribbling and said, "You have obligated yourself to take care of him. Are you familiar with co-dependency?" I scanned my brain for the clinical definition of co-dependency.

I have a BA in Psychology. Why don't I know this? I uttered, "No."

Then she said, "Your assignment is to do some research on co-dependency, and we will talk about it in our next session." She didn't scribble again. I smirked as I keyed CO-DEPENDENCY into my internet search engine. I did not believe this assignment was going to be helpful.

"Why am I researching this? This is a waste of time." I said to myself.

According to Merriam-Webster's Dictionary, "co-dependency is a psychological condition or a relationship in which a person is controlled or manipulated by another who is affected with a pathological condition."

"I don't have this issue. He doesn't manipulate me." I thought to myself.

Next, I found a few articles that described co-dependency. The examples were describing my life, and I was beyond angry. I was angry at him for putting me in this position. I was angry that the therapist dared to suggest that I signed up for the abuse. I was angry at everyone in the world except the one person who had the choice to participate in all of this, me.

It was me who ignored all the red flags. It was me who told myself that he only raped me at gunpoint because he was drunk. I spoke of abusive episodes with comedic flair as opposed to owning the severity of them. I often sat weeping and shivering in my closet while blasting Pavarotti's Romantic Arpeggios because I was so broken. Therapy set me on a path to self-discovery that I had not anticipated.

After several sessions, I decided she had taken me as far as she could on my journey. I began to foray into personal development and meditation. I knew that the frenzied, crazy state of being that I subscribed to had to be deactivated. It was not until years later that I finally had the breakthrough that I so desperately needed. One day (before meditating), I asked the question of "Why did I choose him?" I was driving later that day, and I had an epiphany. He was never my soul mate, he was my wound mate.[1]

The wounds and brokenness I desperately needed to heal in him were really my own wounds manifesting before my eyes. We both had deep abandonment issues. Instead of aggressively taking care of the four-year-old Jennifer that was operating in pain veiled in confidence, I broke myself even more to help him when he NEVER ASKED me to heal him. I protected him (i.e., never reported him to the police) because I wanted him to make me feel safe and protected. How dare I be angry at him when I freely chose to sacrifice it all because I told myself he needed the sacrifice? He never asked me to do any of it. I gave him

---

[1] Wound mate is a person with whom you share a connection over unresolved emotional problems.

everything along with my foolish loyalty because I thought it would show him how he should love me.

I was mad at myself for being loyal to someone who didn't love me enough, and even madder at myself for trying to justify my decision to continue to love him. Step by step, I began to realize that my decision to enter into and maintain toxic relationships (romantic, family, or friendship) was solely based on my failure to heal before opening myself to love. People with abusive behaviors can come and go, but it was up to me to decide to engage or wish them blessings as I walked away.

This revelation gave me the keys to a new life. I live a peaceful life with peaceful relationships. My heart was opened to receive healthy love and empowered to know when to remove people or situations from my life that didn't serve me or support the essence of who I am. In my new life, I wear the power of choice like a badge of honor because I earned it.

Jennifer Hardy is the host of the Boss Your Chaos podcast. She is a certified mindset coach that focuses on life balance strategies and belief breakthroughs. Through her experiences, Jennifer has created a methodology for recognizing opportunities for growth and mindset shifting in the midst of chaos.

She is a "heart agent" who believes that the heart speaks truth, and that truth gives rise to power. Jennifer is also a Real Estate attorney that lives in metro Atlanta, Georgia, with her husband and daughter.

Instagram: **@bossyourchaos**
Website: **www.bossyourchaos.com**
Email: **bossyourchaos@gmail.com**

• CHAPTER 16 •

I Am Okay with Me

I have no recollection of the incident that almost killed me, but the scars I received are constant reminders of just how dark my life was at the time. Either way, September 1, 2016, was the day my life changed forever. My addiction to drugs had finally gotten the best of me and left me confined to a hospital bed for thirty-seven days. The earliest memory that I have during that time was day thirteen. I am sure of that because I posted on Facebook informing my followers that I was in the hospital with a shattered left leg, a fractured right one, six broken vertebrae, road rash up and down my body, and a bald spot in the back of my head. Well, I didn't exactly mention the bald spot.

I remember waking up to a horrific sight. I was shocked to see two very long steel rods placed parallel to each other, protruding through the top of a white cast, on my left leg. The rods were secured by a third rod, running through the heel of my foot, holding my shattered leg together—my right leg in a boot. I was informed by doctors that surgery to finish the ORIF Surgery, which had begun on the day I arrived in the trauma ER, had been put off because of the swelling and huge blisters on my foot.

My upper body was covered in what is called a "clamshell brace," a device that wraps around your back, chest, and stomach area because of the broken vertebrae. It prevented me from bending forward or backward, to prevent further damage. I had spent the first seven days in ICU, and a total of thirty-seven days in the hospital, after having fallen asleep at the wheel, and hitting two utility poles, flipping, and being ejected from my Nissan X-Terra. The bald spot came from me hitting my head on the concrete. I was so high off of Xanax that doctors had to intravenously feed me with more milligrams of the drug to keep my body from going into shock and sedate me.

I desperately tried to leave the hospital to attend my sister/cousin/bff's, Lakeland's wedding, which was scheduled to take place two days later. My mom told me that I was in surgery for hours and that doctors were not sure if I would make it. I was devastated that I missed the wedding that I had helped Lakeland plan. She died four months later of colon cancer.

The weeks leading up to my accident were a blur. I was in what is considered a Psychosis Episode, a symptom of Bipolar disorder. October of 2014 to January 2017, I had experienced a student being killed at our homecoming game, which in turn led me to organizing a gang truce. I lost two uncles, my grandmother, my grandfather, and my co-worker/friend was killed by her ex-boyfriend. Then Lakeland being diagnosed with Stage 4 colon cancer caused me to spiral downward and crash and burn.

As months passed, Lakeland's cancer progressed. I refused to let my cousin see me when I was in the hospital. I didn't think it would be good for either of us to see each other in those conditions. Besides, the chemo was wearing her down, and she didn't have the energy to come and visit me. I understood. I was confined to a wheelchair after being released from the hospital, so our time was sparse. I didn't want her to see me in my chair. She would've been worried about me, and she didn't need that stress, but that didn't keep us from regular video chats.

I could hear the weariness in Lakeland's voice. She also began to express how exhausted she was, which she never did. She was such a positive spirit and always remained optimistic. Lakeland died in January of 2017. I made it to see her in hospice. I was in my wheelchair, but I got close enough to talk to her in her ear. I was allowed to do so alone and in peace. I found out the next morning that she had passed via Facebook.

After Lakeland transitioned, the road ahead of me would be a long one, but my accident, being in a wheelchair, and losing someone very close to me, was the wake-up call that I needed. I had to go through weeks of rehabilitation with my leg. I had to learn how to walk again, but this time with rods and screws in my leg. I was released from doctor's care in May, and by August of 2017, I had made up in my mind that enough was enough. I was tired of feeling sorry for myself and constantly allowing other people to control how I felt about myself. I was sick of living my life, depending on a substance as my coping mechanism.

I no longer wanted to be held captive by my circumstances. I had finally decided that I was tired of standing around drinking poison, waiting on the people who previously hurt me to die. I entered rehab for the umpteenth time, but this time was different, I wanted to live. I had finally grasped my purpose and reasoning for all the pain that I had endured in my life. This time I stayed. I surrendered. I no longer needed to run. I was no longer angry. I was worn, tired, hopeless, and helpless. It was then that I let go and let GOD.

I spent six months in rehab and shut off the outside world. I didn't care about friends, money, or even family. It was life or death for me. I had spiraled out of control and knew better. The intense therapy that I received allowed me to lay all of my burdens on the floor. I laid that stuff down and haven't picked it back up since.

Reka Jones is a native of Atlanta, GA. and is an advocate for Mental Wellness and Recovery. She is a certified Addiction Recovery Empowerment Specialist and works in mental health and substance abuse. She is a person in long-term recovery and states that she likes to think of herself as "The Hope Dealer."

Reka is the creator and Co-Host of the "Always1HunnidShow." She enjoys spending time with her granddaughter, writing, and traveling. She has one son and assists him with his film company, Qfilmz.

"During the midst of my storms, I have learned to dance in the rain"- Reka J.

• CHAPTER 17 •

Secure Your Own Mask Before Helping Others

For six months, I drove to work with a brewing headache. Upon arrival, I felt sick, and my head was banging. I had time to gather my things and pray myself through the day before opening the door and vomiting in the bushes Every-Single-Day. I rinsed my mouth with water, sucked in my stomach, and erected myself. I walked through the door, issuing smiles and good mornings.

That's not how it started. I was so excited to be working after four-months of unemployment. I was confident because I worked with this manager before my lay-off. My mind sighed from relief like I hit the reset button. It made sense that I was self-assured because I'd done it before, and hell, I'm the superstar! That's the reason he called me back! No sweat, right? Wrong! Wrong! Wrong! I ignored the signs saying he was a different person. I erased the memory of his dismissive response when I reached out after my layoff. I shushed my intuition, saying he was rude and callous then, and he would likely be that way if I accepted the job. When he later emailed, offering the job, all of the excuses invoked when returning to a bad relationship became logical.

Hindsight is 20/20, however foresight fuels perfect vision. I crashed in this role because I didn't trust my vision. I started to realize that he was in over his head, and we were not functioning well as a team. Honestly, I wasn't "functioning." I was flatlining. I became ill and felt paralyzed with the fear that everything I touched would perish. I smiled at my friends and family, only scratching the surface of how low I truly felt. I never shared that I decided my son had so many people who love him that he would be fine without me.

I convinced myself that I was not the right mother for him. Even after 1 Samuel 1:27-28 delivered him to me, God's word must've been wrong. I couldn't see the times when God literally reached down and hand-delivered miracles of mercy to me. One morning, after I dropped off my son at daycare, I had a car accident, running into the back of a woman driving an infant in a rear-facing car seat. It was my fault, and I had no explanation. I literally blacked out. I was hysterical and was having an out-of-body experience. I ran to the woman's car and saw my son's face on her baby! The mother called her husband to tell him what happened and ushered me back to my vehicle. In a few minutes, she walked back to ask for my number in case she needed to call me. She told me she and her baby were fine. Then, she walked away, and I never heard from her again. That was God's favor!

In the midst, I allowed a family member to move in, as she was in flight from two other family members' homes. She and I had grown close and spent hours talking frequently. Our conversations were mostly driven by all the negativity in her life and how it victimized her. She laid the blueprint for each toxic relationship to support why she wasn't at fault. I didn't realize I was drawing nearer to "the light" of pity. It was easy to do because I felt like I was helping her in some way.

That feeling overshadowed the marred self-portrait stored in my brain's attic. I felt like I was needed, and that being around me was beneficial. My mind used my late mother's memory to chain my heart to the situation, and again, I ignored the signs. You would think that through everything I was living, I wouldn't have mental space to take in someone. Honestly, I was seeking shelter from myself.

Driving home from the job from hell, she called me in tears, like many times before that day. My mind reconciled that she sounded different. I needed to support my next move and prove my worth. I don't remember much of what she said except, "Can I come and stay with you until I figure out what to do?" I didn't hear her say, "This is the third time I'm running into another situation. I am not holding myself accountable for being the common denominator." That was the Tuesday before my son's 4th birthday. By Friday, I had rearranged his entire room, his only space in the house, and helped her invade it.

The three of us started out enjoying the family unit, but through my rosy lenses, I didn't see how I blew up my son's organized schedule to accommodate someone else. When I invoked adult requirements, like take care of yourself and clean up after yourself, we hit a snag. When my expectations were not met, I was immediately irritated, but I did not effectively communicate my issues. I copped an attitude and set the tone for my house. I dissolved my desire to make a difference and feel needed.

During a very intense verbal altercation, the final straw was when she told me that I had nothing she wanted and had not given her anything. That resonated because I realized that I was fully exposed without securing my mask. I fell to my knees and asked God to reveal why I deserved this plight. Staring at that marred self-image, I bellowed, "GOD! HELP ME! DON'T LEAVE ME HERE!" I pleaded with Him to tell me why I went through that. The next day she was gone, and the answer was clear.

Secure your own mask before you try to help others. Don't panic, expecting others to secure your joy, approval, and clarity. I realized my mask wasn't secured because I couldn't breathe. The pressure was so high that I literally could…not…breathe.

Self-proclaimed "Spiked Cajun Peach," born in Tennessee, raised in Louisiana and Georgia, Marvette Davis is an IT professional in banking. She is the owner of *YIMI Boutique* ™, an online handmade accessories boutique. A true lover of all things creative, she appreciates "Can you make this?" requests.

Marvette contributed to this anthology, settling her heart and mind, and dissolving negative energy. The story told by Davis in this book is a true account of life experiences during tumultuous times. She believes that being true to yourself and others is the best way to elude ambiguity.

Her prayer is that telling her story will touch others. Adding "published author" to her list of accomplishments has been a long-time dream. Friends and family often refer to Marvette as a great storyteller. Her most important life decision is unequivocally adopting her son Gavin. Currently, they live in the metro Atlanta area.

• CHAPTER 18 •

Around this Mountain

One of my favorite childhood songs was "She'll Be Coming 'Round the Mountain When She Comes." It is funny how things speak to you, have a way of warning you, and providing guidance in this life journey. I dreamed my husband and I would have three children, Todd Jr., Ross, and Savannah. Faithful to the dream, our first child was Todd Jr. It was a difficult pregnancy. I was sick daily due to preeclampsia and required many hospital stays.

Just like my dream, Ross was my second gentle baby. We became pregnant a third time, and this time we were expecting Savannah. My dream was clear, and I told everyone we would have three children. Like my first pregnancy, the sickness was daily, yet something was different. My care team dismissed my observations, as each pregnancy is different. My ultrasound revealed that the baby was a boy. A boy? But how, my dream, three children, TJ, Ross, and Savannah. I felt unsure, embarrassed, and even questioned God. I was sure of the dream, but I just did not know the path.

After the ultrasound, I had a vivid dream. It warned about a package and preparations to turn it over. It also warned about not looking at women dressed in black. I awoke and was strangely calm but perplexed. What did it mean? It was too striking not to have a message. My sickness continued, and a week after the dream, I realized I had not felt this baby move. The baby had died, and I would need to deliver. I was heartbroken.

In accordance with my vision, TJ, and Ross, my first two sons were born with only 8-10 hours of labor. My third son, Luke Gabriel, was born after 27 hours of hard labor, stillborn. My body did not handle the stress of the labor. I think back to the dream. The tiny package was the baby. The women in black symbolized death. The strict instructions to make it past the woman in black was my pathway to life again. I always knew that I would have three living children. I did not see around the mountain that Luke, would be my angel baby. This experience rocked my faith, but it did not make me doubt God.

We spent much time in prayer over what God intended us to learn through this experience. First, He is good even in despair. Second, He is sovereign to bless and provide as He sees and still make good on His promises. Third, I am not in control of everything, and the children that we are privileged to birth belong to Him. I was here to love, steward, and point them to God. I learned first-hand that God is in control.

A year later, we tried again. It began with the daily morning sickness. My blood pressure was elevated, and labs showed that some things were a little off. The ultrasound revealed that I was carrying another boy. My heart sank. God did not show me another boy child. I knew I would be headed around the mountain again. Months passed, and like deja vu, the baby didn't move. Again, there was swelling around the heart and brain, but the baby was still alive. Two days later, my fourth son Tyler Wesley passed after another difficult 26-hour delivery.

"Lord, what am I to learn this time?" The first trip around the mountain was a lesson for me; God is sovereign. The second trip was a lesson for others; He is good and trustworthy. It showed people how to love despite the hurt, and how to keep family and marriage strong during a tragedy.

I chased after God for three years after Tyler. I reminded Him of His promise to me. We lived through our pain, shared our healing, and believed Acts 27:25, "Therefore take heart, men, for I believe God, that it will be just as it was told me." I believed God.

Three years later, we were pregnant and had not discussed trying to get pregnant again with doctors. Everyone who loved us was concerned and even mad that we would do this again, risking my health, our happiness, and our stability. We were pregnant again and believing God to deliver His promise, Savannah.

The pregnancy started just like the others with the sickness, three appointments weekly, and injections twice a day. Eight weeks into the pregnancy, we confirmed that the baby was a girl, Savannah. I finally felt like I was heading up the mountain instead of around it. The early tests revealed she would have complications, possibly Down Syndrome, possibly developmental delays. People questioned if I would still carry the baby to term. Fear consumed me and I worried that she would die stillborn, but we clung to faith and prayer.

At 24 weeks, the uneasy feelings returned. My body was not dealing with this pregnancy. I began complaining to my medical team and tests were ordered. Some doctors dismissed my assessment, but others listened and probed deeper. I was at the doctor every other day. One specialist told me I would be a mother soon even though I was 24 weeks. She advised me to think about parenting a preemie. At 25 weeks, I complained, "It is happening again!" I could feel the baby slowly fading away. I knew something was wrong. There were signs of swelling building around her heart. It was clear that things were not improving, and we delivered at 26 weeks. Savannah was born May 5, 2006, 1 pound 9 ounces and our promise was complete.

Trust God, even when He is untraceable. Accept His sovereignty and appeal for all He has for you in this life. Persist around the mountain and search God for the answers and guidance as you travail. There is a path for each of us, and it is not promised to be smooth, easy, and straight to the top. Call upon the Father to help you. Give praise and be patient until the path and direction are clear. Trust that He will do what He says and deliver you to the place He intends, even if it requires several trips around the mountain.

Tiffany Bryant is a first-time writer inspired to share her faith and story of perseverance in "Around this Mountain Again." Her trials of the journey to motherhood, the completion of family through faith, and experiences in a flawed healthcare experience have led her to pursue a Women's Health and Community-based Health Education career.

Tiffany is wife and mom to the Bryant Clan (three children, a dog, and a horse). When she isn't writing or teaching, she enjoys her backyard garden, food escapes, the tennis courts, spending time with her family, sharing their passions and encouraging them to reach their goals.

• CHAPTER 19 •

The Secret Key: How it Unlocked My New Life

The mystery key I found at the bottom of his briefcase while helping him search for his phone. I didn't know what it was then, but I soon found out that it was the key to unlock all of the unanswered questions that continued to swirl in my head, day in and day out. Once I was sure that he was out of town, I headed across town to check things out for myself. It was a secured building, so I had to check the directory to find out the unit number since I only had a single key.

To my surprise, not only was his name listed on the electronic directory board with his actual first initial and last name, but mine was too. Yes, my first initial and last name was listed in a directory for a place that I had never even laid eyes on. I had to follow a resident into the main doors to gain access to the elevator, since it was a secured building. I took the elevator to the 5th floor and walked around the hallway to get the lay of the land.

I then walked toward the unit that was listed. My heart was beating out of my chest. I was impeccably dressed, with my hair done and my designer bag, just in case I ended up toe-to-toe with the alleged paramour. When I got to the door, I noticed that it was appropriately decorated for the season with a festive sign that read, "Merry Christmas." It was the holiday season, and they had the nerve to have their unit decorated like a happy family would.

I had on a nice coat, sunglasses, and gloves. I used the door knocker to knock on the door, just to make sure that the place was empty. As I took the key from my purse, that key that I had found by mistake and painstakingly rushed to have a copy made just in case; it took all I had to place it gently into the keyhole and turn it. It worked! I opened the door. There I was inside of the most delightfully decorated, nicely furnished residence I had ever seen. It was decorated nicer than our own home. It looked just like a page from Better Homes and Garden Magazine.

The kitchen was small but well-stocked and fully furnished with a coffee Keurig and a mini-bar with a selection of rum, bourbon, gin, and liquors. The cabinets were filled with nice dishes and glasses, not to mention the bar stemware that would make a statement in any home. I opened the dishwasher to find it nearly empty, except for two used wine glasses and a dish or two that likely was used for a dessert they shared the night before.

In the living room was a nice cream leather sectional with a heavy tan throw blanket. It sat on a bear-skinned rug, and in front of it was a stately glass and leather coffee table. A nice, oversized coffee table where photo books were displayed with pictures and stories of summer homes in the Hamptons and the things fairytale vacations are made of. A large flat panel TV was positioned across the room with a sculpted Buddha statue on the wall adjacent to it. There was even a large bamboo plant in the corner by the end of the sofa's sectional portion.

Across the room was a stylish barn door, open with a magnificent floor-length mirror resting on it at an angle. Beyond the barn door was the master bedroom. There was a King-sized bed, perfectly made, with a stark white comforter set and sheets. "Her" side had a satin pillowcase on the pillow. Next to the bed was a nightstand with a small lamp and a picture frame. The two of them, photographed embracing, with a picturesque body of water behind them. Wow! They have even vacationed together. I felt so betrayed. How could I have not known, after all this time?

Next to the bedroom was the closet. One side was his, and the other was hers. His suits were neatly arranged, just as they were at our home. There were shirts on hangers and a few pairs of dress shoes to boot. There was not much on her side, but I noticed a few cute tops and dresses with tags still on them. On the top rack were two pairs of Christian Louboutin pumps. Both of them were exactly my size. I tried them on and thought about taking them, but I chose not to because I was playing the long game and not just trying to pick a small fight. There was also a Céline bag and a Chanel bag still wrapped with tags on the top shelf. Over $15,000 "of our money" that he had spent on this "home wrecker." I was furious!

I couldn't believe the "his and her" luxury monogrammed Turkish Cotton bathrobes hanging side by side in the closet. How lovely, I thought. He and I don't even have matching bathrobes. The knife went through my heart like a dagger. As I walked out of the bedroom, I entered the nicely appointed bathroom with the requisite towels, linens, and toiletries. In the drawer, she had several makeup compacts and tubes of lipstick in various shades. I'll bet she likes to get all dolled up for a night on the town with "my husband." Wow!

On the wall was a beautiful heart-shaped painting that said, "You make my heart smile!" My heart sank!!! I doubled over in two. There was the evidence. My husband of twenty years had another woman, with another fully furnished and decorated house, with a totally separate life, all on the other side of town! He was living a DOUBLE LIFE!

All of my emotions rushed in on me at the same time. I was in denial--this can't be true. Is someone playing a cruel joke on me? I was angry, thinking how could he do this to me? I wondered what I had done to deserve this cruel treatment and what I could have done differently to make things better. All I knew for sure is that God did not create me to be emotionally abused, and this was not okay! I deserved better!

I walked out onto the small balcony that overlooked the busy main road, and I shouted, "It's over! I deserve so much more!!" I turned around and walked out of that gut-wrenching residence, never to look back. I called my attorney and set up her next available appointment to get my divorce started. And that is how I used "the mystery key" to unlock my amazing new life!

 Chiquita T. Dent is a Transformational Divorce Coach who helps women increase their self-worth, self-confidence, and self-sufficiency to re-build their brand after experiencing a tough divorce. Chiquita's personal and corporate branding experience, business education, and personal triumph in her own divorce make this work particularly powerful.

She holds a B.S in Business Administration from The School of Business and Industry at Florida A&M University and an MBA from Clark Atlanta University. Chiquita lives in Atlanta, GA, with her amazing teenage son.

CHAPTER 20

Finding Me...One Unexpected Adventure after Another

My story is one about a young woman evolving to live a life of passion and purpose through a series of interesting twists and turns. My unexpected adventure took a pivotal turn when I competed in the Mrs. Ohio America pageant. I had never previously considered doing such a thing because my insecurities were far too great. None of that insecurity was mitigated by graduating at the top of my high school class and earning multiple full scholarships for both undergraduate and graduate school.

After graduate school, I was working as a finance manager when I entered the Mrs. Ohio pageant. There, I met another competitor from my area. As the only women competing from our city, we quickly became friends. Soon, we started discussing our bucket lists which we were determined to execute together. First, we tried out for the Cincinnati Bengals NFL Cheerleading squad. This was a pretty tall order for me. Even though I had won the Mrs. Ohio pageant and was a finalist in the national competition, I was still terrified and insecure about cheering. Without her in my corner, I never would have attempted it. Nevertheless, we persevered and made the team! We cheered our rookie season together and had an absolute BLAST!

In life, we have defining moments. They frequently appear unexpectedly and all too often, tragically. During these times, both character and purpose are revealed. Little did I know that this particular connection was going to be just that. Unbeknownst to me, my friend had survived cancer several years earlier. And unimaginable to anyone, her cancer recurred at the end of our rookie season. A couple of months later, at the age of 28, she was gone. As one can imagine, this completely rocked my world.

Afterward, I spent a lot of time thinking about what I wanted to do and how I could overcome my insecurities to pursue my passion. I knew that my friend would not want me to waste time being scared or feeling undeserving of living a life filled with joy and purpose. After speaking at my teammate's memorial service, I vowed to live life with passion and enthusiasm.

A few months after I experienced my friend's death, I resigned from my position as a finance manager as it was never really my passion. Next, I entered the world of modeling and acting. I was featured in a variety of national, regional, and local projects. Just like my entry into the pageantry and cheer spheres, I was nervous, doubted my ability to be successful, and thought of all the ways it could go wrong. But with a lot of support, I decided to go for it. It wasn't eradicating fear that allowed me to do so, rather embracing the uncertainty and the resolve to proceed down that path anyway. Now that I had my newly discovered confidence and positive outlook, I was ready to take on the next new adventure...or was I?

My husband has had a long career in corporate finance. During his journey, there have been many relocation opportunities for different assignments, as the company has a large global presence. When it was our turn, we first moved to the San Francisco Bay Area, where my passion for health inspired me to become a nurse practitioner. I explored educational opportunities in the area, but unfortunately the programs were just too expensive. Though disappointing, this would just end up a dream delayed because shortly after that, we uprooted our lives again and moved back to Cincinnati.

With two small children in tow, I entered nursing school, earned my Bachelor of Science degree in nursing, worked as an ICU nurse, earned my Master of Science in nursing, and became a nurse practitioner. I was elated to begin my career as a health care provider! But as soon as I became licensed, my husband was relocated to Toronto. Due to differing requirements, the licensing process was significantly more difficult than I could have imagined. As I reflect on my symptoms, I was likely sub-clinically depressed at that time. After having worked so hard to get to that point, to really find ME, and not being able to do what I believed to be my life's calling was heartbreaking.

Though I was always insecure and a bit of an overachieving perfectionist to compensate for that, I had been able to achieve success in each of my endeavors. This time was proving to be far more difficult. To make a long story short, I worked for two and a half years to get my nursing license in Canada. But in literally the same week I was offered my first nurse practitioner job in Canada, my husband was relocated back to Cincinnati. I. Was. Devastated. I wasn't ungrateful, but I was certainly upset that my opportunity to find "me" was snatched away again.

At this point, I have had a variety of career opportunities and disappointments. I have moved multiple times, and supposedly I'm here to stay. We'll see… As I bring this story to the present time, I can say I finally made it to my destination. I'm happily working as a nurse practitioner and serving my community. I have also recently launched a business devoted to improving the health outcomes of black women, and I love all of it. The way my life has worked out so far, I never know how long this will last. But for however long I get to do this, I promise to give it my all.

In pressing through insecurity and disappointment, I learned some important lessons. 1) Adversity can breed resentment, or it can birth resilience. YOU choose which you will embrace. 2) Don't be afraid of life's "unexpected adventures." Life is too short NOT to live your dreams. With this publication, I can say I just added author to my list, and who knows what's next? So, get up and be YOUR best self! You got this, sis.

Marcy Davis Fitzgerald is a nurse practitioner residing in Cincinnati, Ohio. The former pageant queen and NFL cheerleader has worked in corporate finance and holds an MBA from the University of Michigan and a BS in information systems from FAMU.

She founded "Our Health in Focus," an organization to improve the health outcomes of black women. A wife and mother of two active sons, she balances her professional and personal life with her community service endeavors. Through sharing her diverse experiences, she hopes to inspire others to embrace change and live passionately with purpose.

Made in the USA
Monee, IL
17 April 2021